Guitar Today provides you with a thorough introduction to note reading, scales, chords, music fundamentals and *pickstyle*—and *fingerstyle*—playing techniques. Solo and lead playing, as well as accompaniment and rhythm guitar techniques, are presented in a variety of musical styles which include pop, rock, classical, Latin, country, folk

GUITAI TODAY

BOOK ONE

BY JERRY SNYDER

MW01132531

dealer or directly from the publisher. This book is also designed to be used simultaneously with **Bass Today** (#353). Guitar classes can now include the electric or acoustic bass.

CONTENTS

There are two versions of each title on the CD: 1) a duet; 2) an accompaniment part to play the solo part with.

ISBN 0-7390-0809-9 (Book)
ISBN 0-7390-0808-0 (Book and CD)
ISBN 0-7390-0811-0 (CD)

Cover guitars courtesy of **McCabe's Guitar Shop**, Santa Monica, CA.

TYPES OF GUITARS

You can learn to play the guitar using any one of several types of guitar: *steel string acoustic, nylon string classical, solid body electric,* or a *semi-hollow body electric.* The important thing is that the guitar be properly adjusted for ease of playing. The most critical adjustment is the so-called "action." Action refers to the height of the strings above the fingerboard. If the action is too high, the guitar will be difficult to play. The gauge of the strings on the guitar also contributes to the ease of playing. Gauge is the diameter of a string measured in thousandths of an inch. For example, the 1st string can vary in string gauge from .008 (light) to .014 (heavy). A guitar with high action and heavy strings will discourage even the most enthusiastic beginner. Make certain that in the beginning, your acoustic or electric steel string guitar has light gauge strings on it and if you are playing a nylon string classical, I would recommend light, normal or medium tension strings.

As a beginner, the selection of a guitar is a matter of personal preference. The primary difference between the various guitars is *tone quality.* Competitive prices have brought both acoustic and electric guitars into the range for the beginner.

fig. 1   Steel string guitar.

Acoustic Guitars unamplified

STEEL STRING GUITAR. Manufacturers also describe this guitar as a *flat-top guitar* or a *folk guitar.* The body of the guitar is hollow with a flat top, a round soundhole, a pin type bridge, and a pick guard. The neck is fairly narrow and normally joins the body at the 14th fret. The tone quality is bright, brassy, and forceful, and lends itself perfectly to folk, country, ragtime, blues, and pop styles. Beginners should put light gauge strings on their steel string guitar for ease in playing. Bronze strings with ball ends are recommended. The guitar can be played with a pick, with the fingers, or with the thumb and finger picks, fig. 1.

NYLON STRING CLASSICAL GUITAR. Referred to as the *nylon string guitar, classical guitar* or *folk guitar,* this guitar is strung with nylon strings. This contributes to the ease of playing it. The body is hollow with a flat top, it has a round soundhole and a stationary loop type bridge. The neck is wider than that of a steel string guitar. One of the distinguishing characteristics of this guitar is its open peghead. The tone quality might be described as dark, mellow and delicate. This guitar has a rich repertoire of classical music but is also suited for pop, folk, latin, and jazz. The nylon string guitar is played fingerstyle; that is, the strings are plucked with the fingers of the right hand. Never put steel strings on a nylon string guitar, fig. 2.

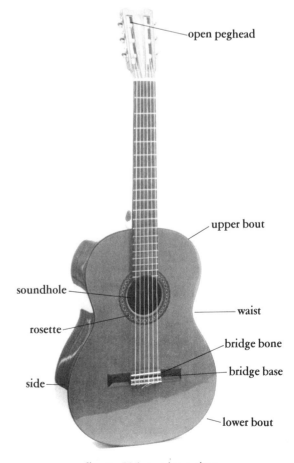

fig. 2   Nylon string guitar.

ACOUSTIC/ELECTRIC GUITARS. The acoustic steel and nylon string guitar have also gone electric. The *acoustic/electric guitar* is the best description for what is now possible with the use of various magnetic, contact, and transducer type pick-ups which amplify the sound. Some of these pick-ups can be attached to the guitar and some are actually built into the guitar.

Electric Guitars

SOLID BODY ELECTRIC GUITAR. Without amplification, this guitar is too soft to be heard even for practicing. It relies almost entirely upon the pick-ups and amplifier. The body is solid and comes in a variety of shapes and designs. It has a thin neck and a "cut-away" design to enable the player to play in high positions. In regards to tone quality, there is an emphasis on the trebles (highs); however, a wide variety of tone qualities are possible. There is sustaining power due to the solid body which absorbs less energy from the strings than does an acoustic or semi-acoustic guitar. This is a favorite guitar with blues and rock guitarists.

fig. 3   Solid body electric guitar.

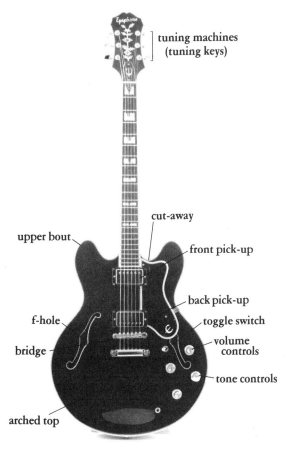

fig. 4   Semi-hollow body electric guitar.

SEMI-HOLLOW BODY ELECTRIC GUITAR. The body of this guitar is thin and semi-hollow. It has an arched top and back, F-holes and a pick guard. The neck is thin and is attached to the body at the 18th fret. This guitar has a wide range of tone qualities ranging from a fairly dark and mellow sound to the more treble sound of the solid body electric. Without an amplifier, this guitar can barely be heard. The semi-hollow body lends itself to country, rock, pop, and blues styles. It has good sustain and can be played at high volumes without feedback problems.

Amplification

A small practice amplifier will be necessary if you begin on an electric guitar. For home practice, a 10 watt amplifier with a 10 inch speaker will be more than adequate. Manufacturers have even smaller practice amps available that may suit your needs. Recently, several companies have developed earphones that can be plugged directly into your guitar. The earphones run on a nine volt battery and are the cheapest solution to hearing your guitar.

RIGHT HAND PLAYING TECHNIQUE

As I mentioned on page 1, this method can be used to learn *either* or *both* PICKSTYLE and FINGERSTYLE guitar technique. Many of today's guitarists play both styles. You have the option in this book to choose one style and skip the other—or learn both. The following is an explanation of the two basic techniques.

Pickstyle

A **PICK**, also called a *flat-pick* or *plectrum*, is used to strum or pick the strings of the guitar. Picks come in various sizes, shapes, and thicknesses, and are made out of many different kinds of material including plastic, nylon, tortoise shell, rubber, felt, and stone. Manufacturers describe the *gauge* or thickness of their picks as light, medium, and heavy. I recommend that beginners use a medium size and thickness pear shape or drop shape pick, fig. 1 and 2.

fig. 1   Pear shape.

fig. 2   Drop shape.

Hold the pick between the thumb and index finger. The pick rests on the top or tip joint of the index finger. Place the thumb over the pick. Press lightly but firmly. The thumb should be kept rigid, fig. 3.

Rest the forearm on the edge of the guitar just above the bridge base, fig. 4.

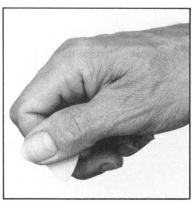

fig. 3   Holding the pick.

fig. 4   Forearm position.

There are three commonly used hand positions: 1) free floating, 2) fanning the fingers, and 3) resting the palm of the hand on the strings behind the bridge. In the free floating position, the middle, ring, and little fingers are curled into the hand. They follow the movement of the thumb and index finger as the hand moves from string to string, fig. 5. Some guitarists fan the fingers and allow the little finger to skim the pick guard, fig. 6. For more stability or for special effects, the palm of the hand can lightly rest on the strings just behind the bridge, fig. 7.

fig. 5   Free floating position.

fig. 6   Fanning the fingers.

fig. 7   Resting the palm.

Down-Stroke

The **DOWN-STROKE** (⊓) is the basic stroke used in pickstyle. In the *down-stroke*, the thumb pushes the pick through the string, stops short of the next string and immediately returns to the starting position. Use an economy of motion. Only follow through enough to finish picking the string. The angle of the pick to the strings should be fairly up-right, fig. 8.

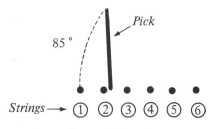

fig. 8   Pick angle.

Fingerstyle

Place the forearm on the edge of the guitar just above the bridge base. Make a fist with your hand. Now open the hand. Keep the fingers in a natural curve. The knuckles should be above the treble strings (strings 3, 2, and 1). Place the thumb on the 5th string. Keep the thumb rigid. Place your index finger on the 1st string, fig. 1 and 2.

fig. 1   Hand position.

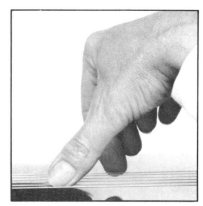

fig. 2   Thumb position.

Rest Stroke

The **REST STROKE** is used to play single note melodies. In this stroke, the index (*i*) or middle (*m*) finger comes to rest on the adjacent (lower sounding) string.

Plant your index finger on the 1st string and your thumb on the 5th string, fig. 3. *Push* the index finger through the string toward the 2nd string. The index finger comes to rest on the 2nd string, fig. 4. The *primary motion* should originate at the joint nearest the hand.

ALTERNATE the index (*i*) and middle (*m*) fingers when you are playing a melody or a single series of notes.

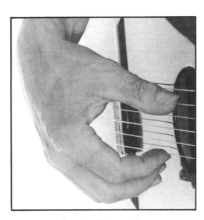

fig. 3   Preparation

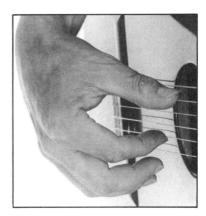

fig. 4   Completion.

LEFT HAND POSITION

An excellent way to develop a good **LEFT HAND POSITION** is to begin by making a fist without bending the wrist. Now bring the hand up to the neck of the guitar and place the fingers on the fingerboard. The wrist should be straight, the fingers curved and the thumb should oppose the fingers in a "grip" position, fig. 5. Most guitarists find their maximum strength when their thumb opposes a spot located between the 1st and 2nd fingers, fig. 6. Depress the string as close to the fret wire as is possible. Avoid cradling the guitar between the thumb and fingers.

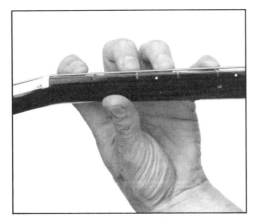

fig. 5   Finger position.

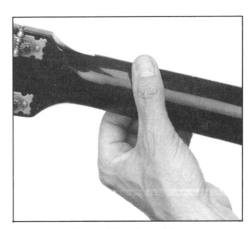

fig. 6   Thumb position.

HOLDING THE GUITAR

Playing positions vary somewhat with the type of guitar, style of music performed, and the right hand technique being used. There are, however, some basic similarities that are important to observe if you are to develop a good left and right hand technique. Study each of the following descriptions.

Sitting Position

Place the waist of the guitar on the right thigh. Tilt the guitar slightly toward you. Keep the neck of the guitar at a 15 degree angle to the floor. Rest the forearm on the edge of the guitar at a point just above the bridge base. Bring the left hand up to the neck of the guitar. The wrist should be kept straight except when playing chords. When you play chords, arch the wrist slightly toward the floor. Never rest the left forearm on your knee or leg, fig. 1.

fig. 1   Sitting position.

Classical Position

A footstool, fig. 2, is used in the classical position to elevate the left knee to a point where it is higher than the hip. Sit forward in your chair and keep the spine straight. Slumping requires more energy than sitting straight. Pull the right leg back under the chair and balance yourself on the ball of your foot. Place the guitar on the left thigh. The guitar will also touch the inside right thigh, the chest, and the right forearm, fig. 3 and 4.

fig. 2   Footstool.

fig. 3   Classical position.

fig. 4   Classical position.

Standing Position

A strap is used to hold the guitar when you are standing. Some guitarists even prefer to use a strap when they are sitting. Acoustic guitar straps are generally attached to a pin on the end of the guitar and the head of the guitar just above the nut, fig. 5. Electric guitars usually have a strap button mounted on the body of the guitar plus the end pin, fig. 6.

fig. 5   Standing position.

fig. 6   Standing position.

TUNING THE GUITAR

Learning to tune a guitar is difficult in the beginning. It is an ear training process that will improve with experience. You are training the ear to match one pitch to another. You are learning to determine whether a string on your guitar is the same, higher or lower than a reference or *tuning pitch*. The *tuning pitch* is the pitch or tone you are attempting to match. It can be provided by a tuning fork (E), a piano, another guitar, a record or by the guitar itself.

TUNING TECHNIQUE. Listen to the *tuning pitch*. Determine whether the string you are tuning is the same, higher or lower than the tuning pitch. If the guitar sounds lower, you must tighten the string to raise the pitch. If the guitar sounds higher, loosen the string to lower the pitch. If you are not sure if the string is higher or lower, purposely tune the string lower. It is generally easier to approach the tuning pitch from a lower sounding pitch than it is to tune down to a pitch. With your left hand gripping the appropriate tuning key, pluck the string with a pick or the thumb as you slowly turn the tuning key. This enables you to hear the pitch change as you are making adjustments to it. Listen to the tuning pitch again. Repeat this procedure until you are satisfied that you have been able to match the tuning pitch.

Tuning the Guitar to Itself

The guitar can provide its own *tuning pitch*. Begin with the 6th string. Either tune it to a tuning pitch provided by some outside source (tuning fork, pitchpipe, piano, record) or estimate the pitch. The pitch of the low E, 6th string usually doesn't vary too much between tunings. Now proceed through the various steps described in fig. 1–5.

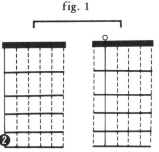

fig. 1

Place the 2nd finger on the 5th fret, 6th string, match the open 5th string to that pitch.

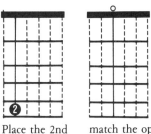

fig. 2

Place the 2nd finger on the 5th fret, 5th string, match the open 4th string to that pitch.

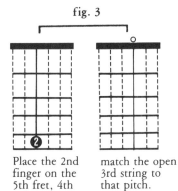

fig. 3

Place the 2nd finger on the 5th fret, 4th string, match the open 3rd string to that pitch.

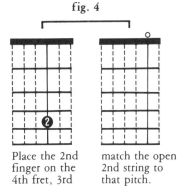

fig. 4

Place the 2nd finger on the 4th fret, 3rd string, match the open 2nd string to that pitch.

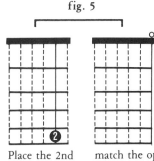

fig. 5

Place the 2nd finger on the 5th fret, 2nd string, match the open 1st string to that pitch.

Tuning to a Piano

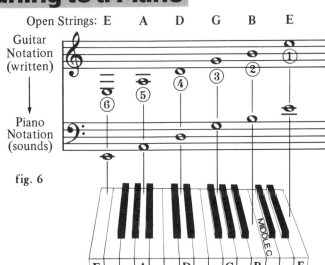

Open Strings: E A D G B E

Guitar Notation (written)

Piano Notation (sounds)

fig. 6

Guitar notation *sounds* an octave (8 notes) lower than written. So when you tune your guitar to a piano, you must be certain that you are tuning the strings to the correct pitch, fig. 6. Play the *tuning pitch* on the piano and then attempt to match the open guitar string to it. Begin with the 6th string.

Electronic Tuners

There are many inexpensive electronic guitar tunings available that will eliminate the tuning problem for you. They have built in microphones for acoustic guitars and a chord input for electric guitars. They are well worth the investment.

MUSIC NOTATION

Notes

In music notation, **NOTES** are the basic symbols used to indicate rhythm. Rhythm refers to the duration, length, or time value given to a note. A **QUARTER NOTE** generally represents the basic beat or pulse in music.

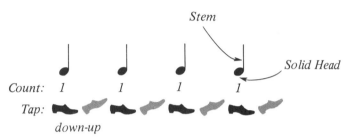

fig. 1   Quarter notes.

QUARTER NOTE. A quarter note receives one count or beat. It has a solid head with a stem attached to the side. Use your foot to *tap* the rhythm of the quarter note. Each note receives a *down* and an *up*.

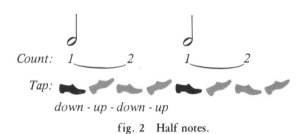

fig. 2   Half notes.

HALF NOTE. A half note receives two counts or beats. It has an empty head with a stem attached to the side. Use your foot to *tap* the rhythm of the half note. Each note receives a *down-up-down-up*.

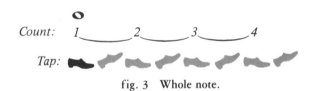

fig. 3   Whole note.

WHOLE NOTE. The whole note receives four counts or beats. This note does not have a stem. Use your foot to *tap* the rhythm of the whole note. Each note receives four *down-ups*.

Bar Lines, Measures and Time Signatures

BAR LINES are used to organize notes into **MEASURES** that have the same number of *beats* in them. The most common placement of bar lines is every four beats. A *double bar line* is used at the end of a song.

The **4/4 TIME SIGNATURE** is the most common *time signature*. The top number indicates how many beats are in a measure. The bottom number tells you what kind of a note receives one beat. The time signature is placed at the beginning of the music. As you *tap* your foot, clap the following rhythm.

$\frac{4}{4}$ = Four beats in each measure
$\frac{4}{4}$ = A quarter note receives one beat

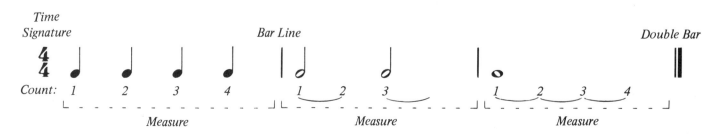

Staff

Notes are placed on a **STAFF** to indicate their *pitch* or *sound*. Pitch refers to the relative high or lowness of a sound. The *staff* has five lines and four spaces (fig. 1). Notes can be placed on a line or in a space, fig. 2 and 3. The higher the note is paced on the staff, the higher the note sounds.

Lines   fig. 1   Staff.   Spaces   fig. 2   Notes on lines.   fig. 3   Notes in spaces.

Clef Sign

A **CLEF SIGN** is added to the music staff to indicate what the notes on the lines and spaces represent. Guitar notation uses a **TREBLE** or **G CLEF**, fig. 4. The 1st seven letters of the alphabet are used to give names to the notes—A, B, C, D, E, F, G. The names of the lines are E, G, B, D, F—Every Good Boy Does Fine. The names of the spaces are F, A, C, E which spells **FACE**.

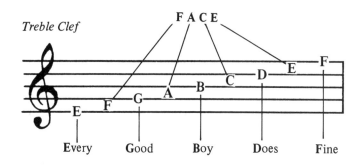

fig. 4   The treble clef and names of lines and spaces.

Frames

FRAMES are used by guitarists to indicate the placement of the *left hand fingers* on the fingerboard. The *frame* represents the strings and frets of the guitar fingerboard, fig. 5. Numbers placed on or above the frame represents the fingers of the left hand. The letter O stands for an open string and an X means not to play the string.

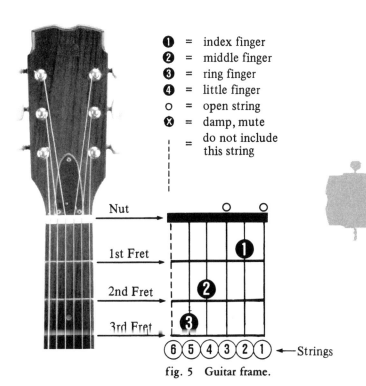

❶ = index finger
❷ = middle finger
❸ = ring finger
❹ = little finger
o = open string
❽ = damp, mute
┊ = do not include this string

fig. 5   Guitar frame.

Tablature

TABLATURE is a six line staff that graphically represents the guitar fingerboard. Numbers placed on the tablature represent the frets of the guitar. The *fret* and *string* of any note can be indicated by placing a number on the appropriate line of the tablature. Tablature is a system of notation often used in rock, country, folk and blues styles of guitar playing, fig. 6.

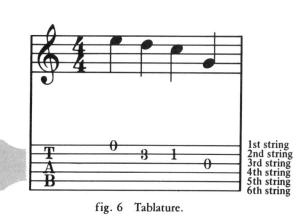

1st string
2nd string
3rd string
4th string
5th string
6th string

fig. 6   Tablature.

NOTES ON THE FIRST STRING

E Open, 1st string

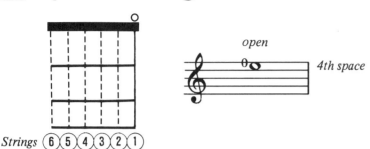

Strings (6)(5)(4)(3)(2)(1)

The 1st string of the guitar is the highest sounding and thinnest string. As you hold the guitar, it is the string nearest the floor. In music notation, the **OPEN E, 1ST STRING** is located on the fourth space of the staff. Open means the string is not fingered.

Before playing exercises 1–3, it will be helpful to review and practice the **PICKSTYLE** and **FINGERSTYLE** right hand techniques presented on pages 4 and 5. Pickstyle players should use a *down-stroke* (⊓) on each note (see page 4). Fingerstyle players should alternate the index (*i*) and middle (*m*) fingers. Use *rest strokes* (see page 5). When playing exercise 1, count out loud and keep a steady beat.

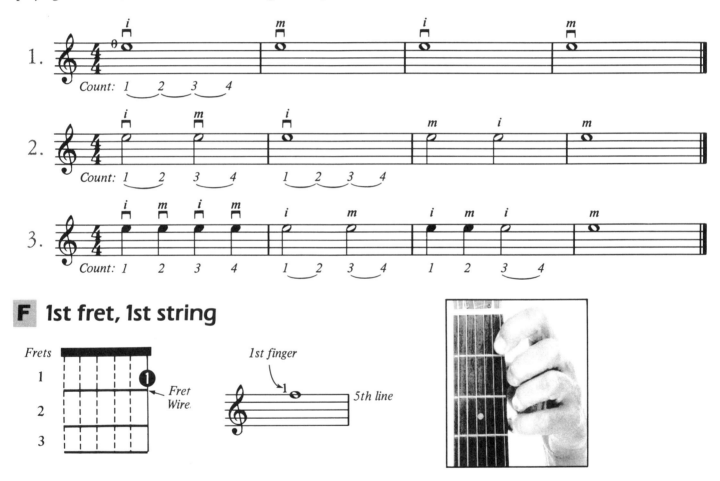

F 1st fret, 1st string

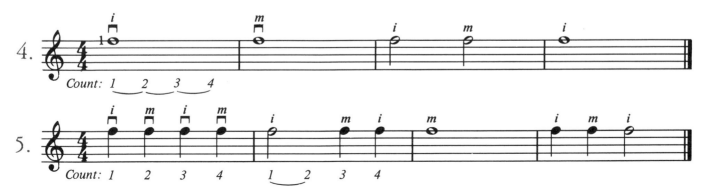

Place the 1st finger of the left hand on the 1st fret as close as possible to the fret wire. The fleshy part of the finger is actually touching the fret wire. Apply pressure just behind the fret wire. In music notation, the F is located on the 5th line of the music staff.

The E and F are now combined in the song *Mist*. You play the **SOLO** or top line. Your teacher or a friend can play the **ACCOMPANIMENT**. This song is eight measures long. When you reach the end of the 1st line continue on to the 2nd line.

MIST

J.S.

*Acc. (Accompaniment) When Acc. or Solo is followed by *, it means the student will be able to play this part later.

G 3rd fret, 1st string

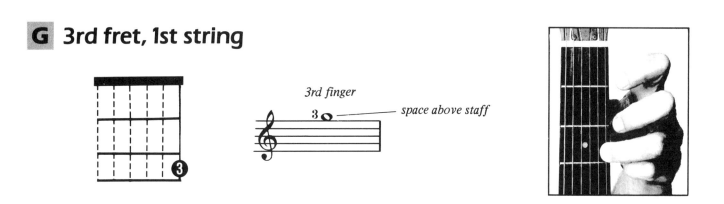

Place the 3rd or ring finger of the left hand on the 3rd fret immediately behind the fret wire. Keep the left hand fingers *spread apart* so that the index finger is above the 1st fret. In music notation, the G is located on the 1st space above the staff.

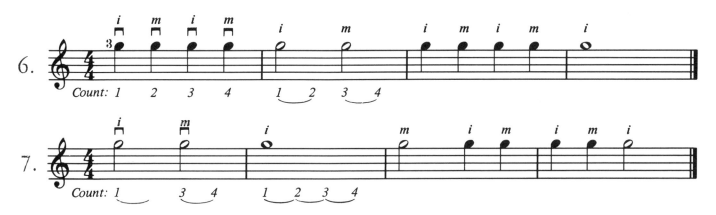

REVIEW: 1st string E, F and G

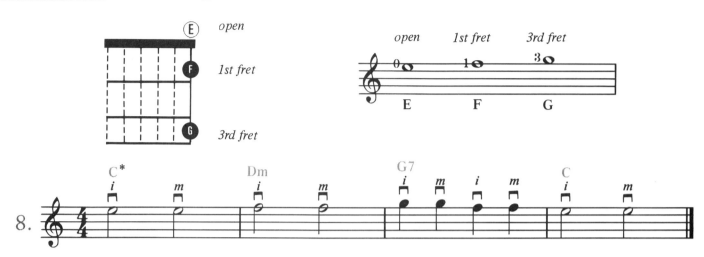

*The gray letters placed above the music indicate chords that can be played by another guitarist.

REVIEW: Right Hand Technique

PICKSTYLE. Continue to play the notes using a down-stroke (⊓) with the pick. The down-stroke sign (⊓) will be eliminated from this point unless it is needed to help clarify the right hand technique.

FINGERSTYLE. Continue to *alternate* the index (*i*) and middle (*m*) fingers using the *rest stroke*. You can begin a song or exercise with either the index or middle finger.

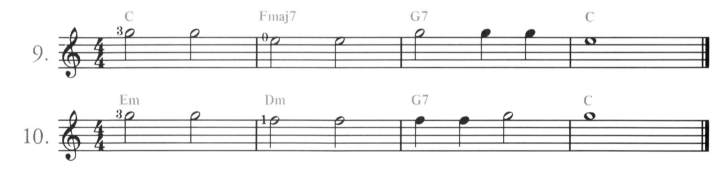

Chelsie uses the 1st string E, F and G. Play the **SOLO** as your teacher or friend plays the **ACCOMPANIMENT**. Play this song at a slow tempo (speed). Keep a steady beat.

CHELSIE

J.S.

NOTES ON THE SECOND STRING

B Open, 2nd string

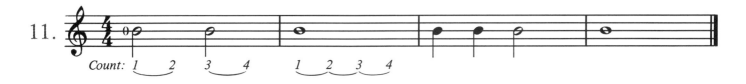

The open 2nd string is tuned to B. In music notation, the B is located on the 3rd or middle line of the music staff.

11.

Count: 1 2 3 4   1 2 3 4

12.

Count: 1 2 3 4   1 2 3 4

C 1st fret, 2nd string

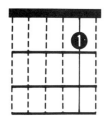

Place the index finger of the left hand on the 1st fret, 2nd string—just behind the metal fret. In music notation, the C is located in the 3rd space of the staff.

13.

B-C MIX

J.S.

Solo

G (arpeggios)   Am   D7   G

Acc.*

D 3rd fret, 2nd string

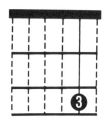

3rd finger

4th line

Place the 3rd finger of the left hand on the 3rd fret of the 2nd string. D is located on the 4th line of the music staff.

14.

15.

16.

17.

REVIEW: Notes on the 1st and 2nd strings

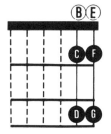

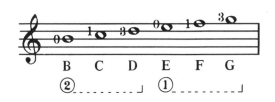

B C D E F G

② ①

Notice that the left hand fingering pattern is the same for both the 1st and 2nd strings. Keep the fingers spread above the frets. The thumb is placed on the back of the neck at a spot that opposes the 1st and 2nd fingers (see page 5).

EASY ROCK

J.S.

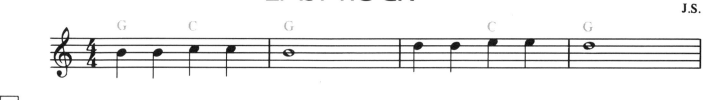

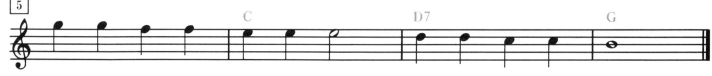

Tempo Markings

TEMPO refers to the *speed* of the music. Three principal tempo markings are *Andante* (slow), *Moderato* (moderately), and *Allegro* (fast).

ROCKIN' ON TWO

Play the SOLO part to *Breezin'*. Eventually, you will be able to play the accompaniment as well.

BREEZIN'

Quarter Rest

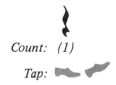

Count: *(1)*

Tap:

QUARTER REST. A rest is a symbol used in music to indicate *silence*. For each note, there is a corresponding rest that has the same time value. A *quarter rest* receives one count or beat. Rests are counted the same way you count notes. A parenthesis placed around the counting indicates that rests are symbols of silence.

18.

Count: *(1)* 2 3 4 *(1)* 2 3 4 *(1)* 2 3 4 1 2 3 4

Repeat Sign

REPEAT SIGNS are used in music to avoid writing out repeated passages of music. The sign consists of two double bars with two dots on the inside, facing the measures to be repeated. Play the measures with the repeat signs twice.

Repeat Sign *Repeat Sign*

19.

Count: *(1)* 2 3 4 1 2 3 4
Rest

COMIN' OUT ROCK

Moderato

Repeat Sign

J.S.

Rhythm Guitar

This is a suggested chord accompaniment for *Comin' Out Rock*. Another guitarist can play this part now. Later, you will be able to play it. Use successive down-strokes on the bass notes and alternate strokes on the chords. Give the 2nd and 4th beats of the measure an accent (>) or emphasis.

Dotted Half Note

Count: 1   2   3

Tap:

DOTTED HALF NOTE. A **DOT** adds one half the value to a note. A dotted half note receives three counts or beats (2 + 1). Count and tap the beats as you play.

3/4 Time Signature

The **3/4 TIME SIGNATURE** organizes the rhythm of music into three beats in each measure. The 1st beat of the measure should receive more emphasis or stress. Count **1** 2 3 | **1** 2 3.

3 = Three beats in each measure
4 = A quarter note receives one beat

PRELUDE

M. Carcassi

Dal Segno

DAL SEGNO or **D.S. means "from the sign." It is one of the signs used in music that directs the player to skip backward through the music to a place marked with a sign (𝄋). *D.S. al Fine* means to go back and play from the sign to the place marked *Fine* (end). In this case, go back to the 2nd line and play it again.

Tie

A **TIE** is a curved line that connects two notes of the *same pitch*. A tie is necessary if you wish to hold a note beyond the bar line. Play the 1st note and hold it for the combined count of the two notes.

SORT OF BLUE

MARY ANN

Some Kind Of Sunset is a Latin jazz song. Learn how to play the solo part. Practice the song slowly at first.

SOME KIND OF SUNSET

J.S.

Incomplete Measure

Songs do not always start on the 1st beat of the measure. They can begin on any beat. When this occurs it results in an **INCOMPLETE MEASURE** at the beginning and at the end of the song.

GENTLE

J.S.

NOTES ON THE THIRD STRING

G Open, 3rd string

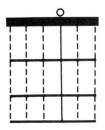
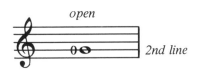

The open 3rd string is G. It is located on the 2nd line of the music staff. When a stem is added to a quarter or half note that is written below the 3rd line of the staff, the stem is attached to the right side and extends above the note head.

A 2nd fret, 3rd string

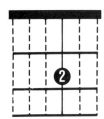

Place the 2nd finger on the left hand on the 2nd fret, 3rd string. In music notation, the A is located on the 2nd space of the music staff.

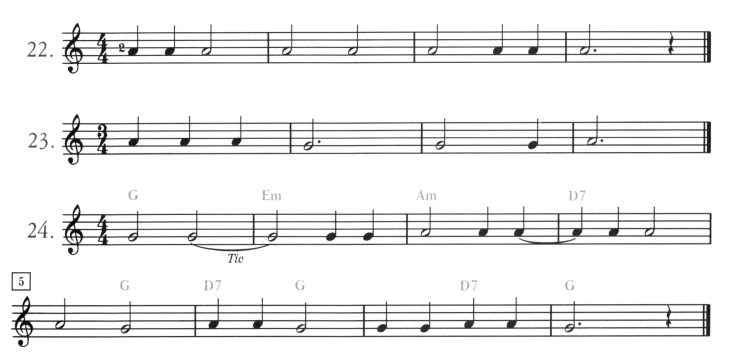

REVIEW: Notes on the 1st, 2nd and 3rd strings

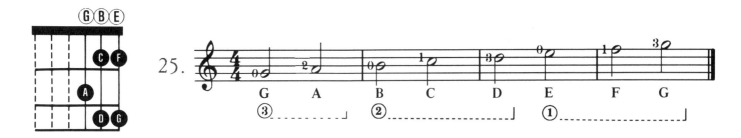

Play the solo part in *Study*. At a later time, you will also be able to play the accompaniment part.

STUDY

N. Coste
adapted by J.S.

FIRST and **SECOND ENDINGS** are another way of directing the player to repeat a section of music. In *Jingle Bells*, play the 1st two lines of music and the *1st ending*. Go back to the beginning and repeat the 1st and 2nd lines of music. Skip the 1st ending and play the *2nd ending*.

JINGLE BELLS

J. Pierpont

Da Capo (D.C.) al Fine

DA CAPO or **D.C.** means "from the beginning." It directs the player to go back to the beginning of the music. *D.C. al Fine* directs the player to return to the beginning of the music and to play to the place marked *Fine* (end). In *Peaceful Feeling*, play the 1st and 2nd lines of music and then repeat them (repeat sign). Now continue on and play the 3rd and 4th lines of music. Observe the *D.C. al Fine* and go back to the beginning of the music. Play the 1st and 2nd lines of music again and end at the *Fine* (the end of the 2nd line).

Practice the solo part in *Peaceful Feeling*.

PEACEFUL FEELING

CHORDS

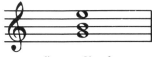

fig. 1 Chord.

When two or more notes are played at the *same time*, it is called a **CHORD**. The notes are placed above and below each other on the music staff and are played together (simultaneously), fig. 1.

There are several techniques used to play chords. You can **STRUM** the strings with a pick, with the thumb and finger, or with the index finger. You can **PLUCK** the strings with the thumb and fingers or with the fingers and a pick. Each technique has a legitimate use and application. It will be valuable for you to eventually learn all of the various right hand techniques.

Strum Techniques

The **STRUM TECHNIQUE** is the easiest to use when you are just beginning to learn how to play chords. Using one of the techniques described below, strum the open 3rd string and then continue *downward* across the 2nd and 1st strings, fig. 2.

Strings

fig. 2 Strum technique.

PICKSTYLE. Strum the strings with a *pick* held between your thumb and index finger. Review page 4. Use a *down-stroke* (⊓) as you strum from the 3rd string toward the 1st string, fig. 3 and 4. In the down-stroke, the thumb *pushes* the pick through the strings. When you have completed the strum, return your hand to the starting position.

fig. 3 Pickstyle preparation.

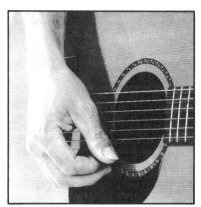

fig. 4 Completion.

FINGERSTYLE. Strum *down* across the strings with the nail of the index finger. Keep the hand above the strings. The motion of the strum is primarily a finger motion, fig. 5 and 6. This type of strum is called *brush, scratch*, or a *finger strum*.

fig. 5 Finger strum preparation.

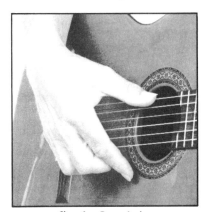

fig. 6 Completion.

The *thumb strum* or *sweep* is done with a straight and rigid thumb. Do not bend the thumb at the 1st joint. Strum downward across the strings (bass to treble). The primary motion is in the wrist with a secondary motion in the thumb as it moves toward the fingers. The sound that you produce with this strum is a combination of flesh and nail (depending on the length of your nail), fig. 7 and 8.

fig. 7 Thumb strum preparation.

fig. 8 Completion.

Plucking Techniques

Plucking the strings rather than strumming the strings is a *fingerstyle* technique developed by classical, folk, and ragtime guitarists. Today, this technique is used in all styles of music: pop, jazz, latin, rock, etc.

Free Stroke

FINGERSTYLE. A FREE STROKE is used to play chords. In the *free stroke*, the fingers and thumb pass over the adjacent strings.

Plant your index finger on the 1st string. The finger should be slightly curved, fig. 1. *Push* the index finger through the string to a spot slightly above and over the adjacent string, fig. 2. The *primary* motion originates at the joint nearest the hand.

Plant the thumb on the 5th string. *Push* the thumb through the 5th string towards the adjacent (neighboring) 4th string, fig. 3. The thumb should pass over and above the 4th string. The *primary* motion is from the joint nearest the hand. Keep the thumb rigid, fig. 4.

fig. 1   Preparation.

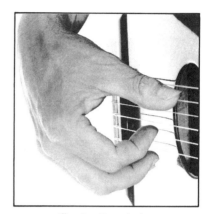

fig. 2   Completion

fig. 3   Preparation.

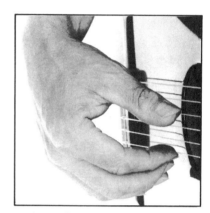

fig. 4   Completion

Playing Chords

In music notation, the right hand fingerstyle technique is indicated in the music by the symbols *p, i, m* and *a: p (pulgar)* = thumb; *i (indice)* = index finger; *m (medio)* = middle finger; *a (anular)* = ring finger

Hand Position. In order to play **CHORDS**, the fingers and the thumb must pluck the strings simultaneously. Place the thumb (*p*) on the 3rd string, the index (*i*) finger on the 2nd string and the middle finger (*m*) on the 1st string. Be certain that the thumb and fingers are not on a collision course. See fig. 2, page 5. The thumb should be rigid and should extend toward the fingerboard of the guitar. Keep the fingers bunched together with the tips touching the strings close to the fingernails. The fingers should be slightly arched, fig. 5.

fig. 5   Hand position.

Technique. Prepare the right hand thumb and fingers to play the chord by placing them on the strings *before* you play the notes. This is called *planting* the hand. It will help you to develop an accurate and consistent technique.

Now that the hand is "planted," *squeeze* the strings until you have *pushed* your fingers and thumb over and above the adjacent strings. The thumb moves toward the 1st string and the fingers move toward the palm of the hand. The primary motion of this *free stroke* is at the joint nearest the hand. Keep the thumb straight and rigid. Do not bend the tip joint, fig. 6 and 7.

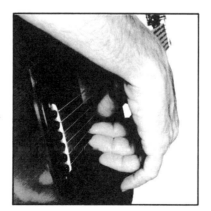

fig. 6   Fingerstyle preparation.

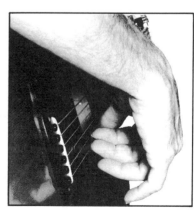

fig. 7   Completion.

Em Chord 3 strings

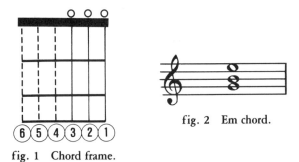

fig. 1 Chord frame.

fig. 2 Em chord.

The **E minor (Em) CHORD** can be played by strumming or plucking the open 3rd, 2nd, and 1st strings of the guitar. A chord frame is often used to notate guitar chords, fig. 1. Dashed lines mean that these strings are omitted from the chord. The letter O stands for *open string* (review page 9). The Em chord is notated in standard music notation in fig. 2.

Pickstyle-Fingerstyle Option

This book is designed to teach the *basics* of the two major right hand styles: *pickstyle* and *fingerstyle*. You have the OPTION of either concentrating on one of the styles or learning them both. If you are studying with a teacher, seek his/her advice for the best approach for you. Most of the material presented can be played using either style. However, some material will demonstrate the advantage of using one technique over the other.

Pickstyle. Play exercises 26 and 27 using a *down-stroke* (⊓) with a pick. Review pages 4 and 24 for an explanation of this technique.

Fingerstyle (strumming). Play exercises 26 and 27 using the *finger strum* or the *thumb strum* described on page 24.

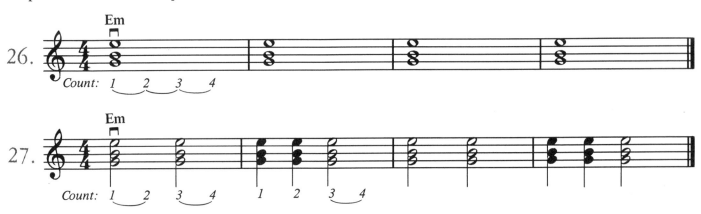

Fingerstyle (plucking). Play exercises 28 and 29 using the plucking technique described on page 25 (free stroke). It is important to place or *plant* the right hand in position before you pluck the strings.

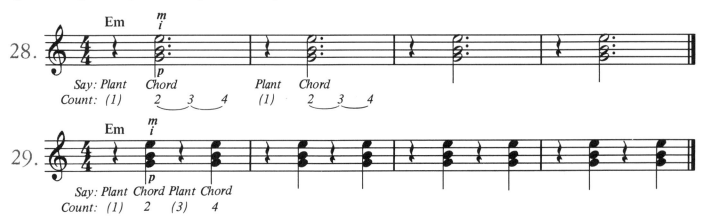

Get in the habit of planting the fingers immediately before plucking the strings. Exercise 30 requires that you plant the hand very quickly.

Play the accompaniment of *Minor Toot* as another guitarist plays the solo. Strum or pluck the top (treble) three strings. Give a little more emphasis or slightly accent (>) the 1st beat of the measure.

MINOR TOOT

J.S.

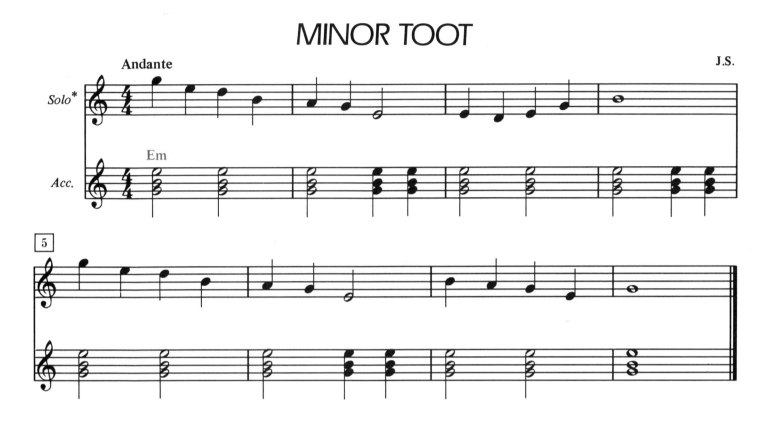

Bass-Chord Accompaniment

A common accompaniment pattern is to play the lowest (sounding) tone in the chord and then to strum or pluck the remaining strings. Play the accompaniment part only to *Night Journey*.

Pickstyle. Play the open 3rd string with a down-stroke and then strum the 2nd and 1st strings.

Fingerstyle. Pluck the open 3rd string with the thumb and then either strum (with the index finger) or pluck the 2nd and 1st strings.

NIGHT JOURNEY

J.S.

C and G⁷ Chords 3 strings

Two additional chords that can be played on the treble strings (strings 3, 2, and 1) are the **C CHORD** and the **G SEVENTH (G7) CHORD**.

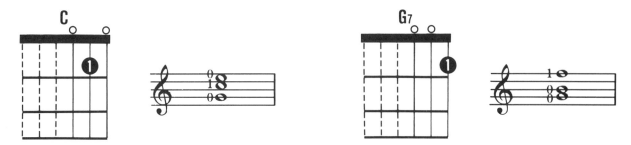

To play the C chord, place the tip of the left hand index finger on the 1st fret, 2nd string. Make certain that you are not touching the 1st or 3rd string. For the G7 chord, depress the 1st string at the 1st fret with the index finger. Practice the following exercise.

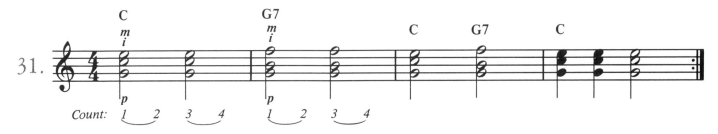

In the *Chord Study*, the student plays the Acc. part.

CHORD STUDY

J.S.

G Chord 3 strings

To play this **G CHORD**, fret the 1st string at the 3rd fret. Use the 3rd or ring finger of the left hand. Strum or pluck the 3rd, 2nd, and 1st strings.

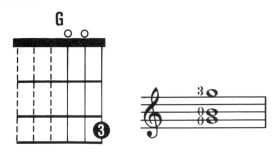

Learn to play the accompaniment part for *Morning Is Come*.

MORNING IS COME

Round

*Invite another guitarist to play this song as a *round*. When the 1st guitar reaches Ⓐ, the 2nd guitar begins the song.

Meditation provides you with a review of the C, Em, G7 and G chords. Play the solo part.

MEDITATION

J.S.

Half Step and Whole Step

The distance between two tones is called an *interval*. The smallest interval is the **HALF STEP**. Guitar frets are placed a *half step* apart on the fingerboard. In the musical alphabet—A, B, C, D, E, F, G—there are two *natural half steps*. They occur between B and C (fig. 1) and E and F (fig. 2).

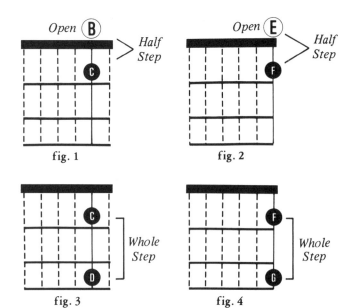

fig. 1   fig. 2

Two half steps (½ + ½) equal a **WHOLE STEP**. All of the other tones in the musical alphabet are a *natural whole step* apart. For example, the interval distance between C and D (fig. 3) and F and G (fig. 4) is a *whole step*. These notes are two frets apart.

fig. 3   fig. 4

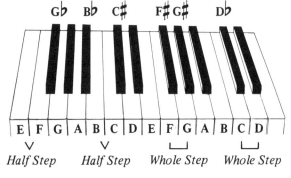

fig. 5   Piano keyboard.

Notes located between the natural whole steps are called **SHARPS** (♯) or **FLATS** (♭). On the piano keyboard, the black keys are sharps or flats, fig. 5. On the guitar, the notes that occur between the natural whole steps are the sharps or flats.

Sharps

When a **SHARP** (♯) is placed before a note in music notation, it *raises* the note one half step higher. On the guitar, that is the distance of one fret, fig. 6.

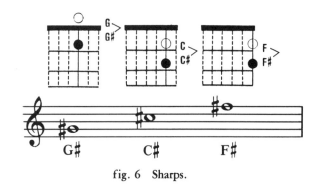

fig. 6   Sharps.

F♯ 2nd fret, 1st string

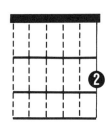

2nd finger

5th line

Place the 2nd finger of the left hand on the 2nd fret, 1st string. The customary practice in music notation is to write the sharp once for each measure. All F's are to be played as F♯ until and up to the bar line. The bar line cancels the sharp so that it must be written in again if there are any F sharps to be played in the next measure. Play the following drill.

33.

D⁷ Chord 3 strings

Arch the 2nd finger when playing the **D7 CHORD** to make certain that it is not touching the 2nd string. Place the fingers just behind the fret wire. If a fretted string does not produce a clear tone, you need to either press more firmly or move the finger closer to the fret wire. The left hand fingernails must be short.

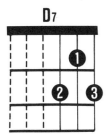

PLAYING TECHNIQUES

Pickstyle. Play the following chord drills using a down-stroke (⊓) with the pick. If you strike the strings near the bridge, you will get a bright treble sound. As you move toward the fingerboard, the tone gets increasingly darker and mellow.

Fingerstyle. Place the thumb on the 3rd string, the index finger on the 2nd string and the middle finger on the 1st string. Pluck the strings simultaneously using the free stroke. You could also strum the chords. Review pages 24 and 25.

GUIDE FINGER. The 3rd finger (⁻3) serves as a *guide finger* when going from the D7 to G chord. It maintains contact with the 1st string as it *slides* from the 2nd to the 3rd fret. There should be no sound as the finger moves along the string. Also use this technique when going from the G to the D7 chord.

COMMON FINGER. The D7 and C chord have a *common finger*. In both chords, the 1st finger is on the 2nd string, 1st fret. Be sure to leave this finger down as you go from the D7 to the C chord.

BASS-CHORD STUDY

For additional practice in playing the G, C and D7 chords, turn back to page 14 and play the chords in exercises 15–17 and the accompaniment part to *Easy Rock*. Strum or pluck a chord on every downbeat in the measure.

Dynamics

DYNAMICS are signs that indicate how loud or soft to play the music. They add interest to the music by adding contrast. Begin by playing *El Coqui* loud (*f*). On the repeat, play the music softly (*p*). Play loud again after the 2nd ending.

piano	*(p)*	Soft
mezzo piano	*(mp)*	Moderately Soft
mezzo forte	*(mf)*	Moderately Loud
forte	*(f)*	Loud
fortissimo	*(ff)*	Very Loud

Practice the solo and accompaniment parts for *El Coqui*. The tempo for this song is *Allegretto*. Allegretto is slightly less fast than Allegro.

EL COQUI

Puerto Rican Folk Song

MAJOR SCALE

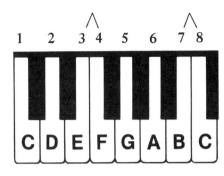

A scale is a series of consecutive tones moving from one tone to another. The **MAJOR SCALE** is the most commonly used scale. The major scale is a series of eight successive tones that have a pattern of whole and half steps. The major scale has a half step between the 3rd and 4th and the 7th and 8th tones of the scale. All other scale tones are a whole step apart. fig. 1.

fig. 1   Keyboard analysis—C major scale.

G Major Scale

In order to obtain the correct pattern of whole and half steps, an F♯ must be added to the **G MAJOR SCALE**, fig. 2 and 3.

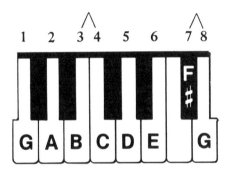

fig. 2   Keyboard analysis—G major scale.

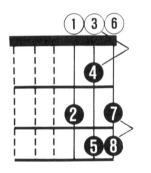 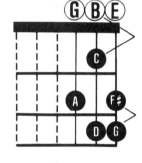

fig. 3   Fretboard analysis—G major scale.

Play the G Major Scale, exercise 37. Notice the *half steps* between the 3rd and 4th and the 7th and 8th tones of the scale. Then play the *G Scale Study*.

G SCALE STUDY

Key Signature

A song based on the G major scale is in the **KEY OF G MAJOR**. Since the F is sharp in the G scale, every F will be sharp in the key of G major. Instead of making all the F's sharp in the song, the sharp is indicated at the beginning, in the **KEY SIGNATURE**. Sharps or flats shown in the key signature are effective throughout the song.

FOLK SONG

French

Principal Chords

The **PRINCIPAL CHORDS** are chords built on the 1st (I), 4th (IV), and 5th (V) tones of the major scale. In the Key of G Major, the principal chords are G, C, and D7. The G chord functions as *home base*. Most songs in the Key of G begin and end on a G chord. The D7 is the next most frequently used chord.

Principal chords in G major

G# 4th fret, 1st string

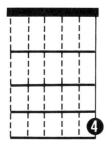

4th finger

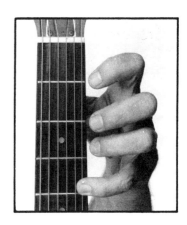

Place the 4th finger (pinky) on the 4th fret, 1st string for the G#. Remember that the sharp only needs to be written once in each measure.

Natural Sign

A **NATURAL SIGN** (♮) is used to *cancel* the effect of a sharp or flat. When placed before a note, it returns the note to its unaltered form.

Leger Lines

LEGER LINES are lines that are added above or below the staff to extend the range. In order to notate the A, 5th fret, 1st string, it is necessary to add one leger line above the staff.

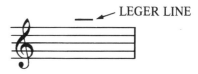

LEGER LINE

A 5th fret, 1st string

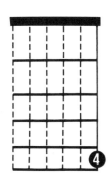

4th finger

In music notation, the A, 5th fret, 1st string is located on the 1st leger line above the staff. Shift the left hand, 4th finger up to the 5th fret. You are now in *2nd position*. It is called 2nd position because the 1st finger is at the 2nd fret.

Shifting

The following exercise gives you some practice in **SHIFTING** the left hand from *1st position* to *2nd position* and back again. *Spanish Song* requires a shift to the 2nd position in order to play the A at the 5th fret.

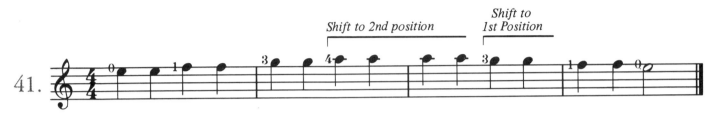

The tempo or speed for *Spanish Song* is indicated as *Adagio*. Adagio is a slower tempo than Andante.

SPANISH SONG

Traditional

*This song is played at an *Adagio* tempo so you could use all down strokes (⊓) with the pick.

OPEN BASS STRINGS

The 4th, 5th, and 6th strings of the guitar are called the **BASS STRINGS**. The open 4th string is the **D** string. In music notation, it is located on the 1st space below the staff, fig. 1. The open 5th string is an A. In order to notate the A, two *leger lines* must be added below the staff. The A is located on the 2nd leger line, fig.2. The 6th string or E string is the lowest note on the guitar. Three leger lines need to be added to the staff to notate E. The E is located on the space below the 3rd leger line, fig. 3.

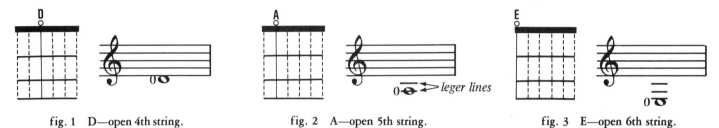

fig. 1   D—open 4th string.   fig. 2   A—open 5th string.   fig. 3   E—open 6th string.

Use either a *down-stroke* (⊓) with a **PICK** or a *free stroke* with the **THUMB**. Review page 25 for an explanation of the free stroke. Check your arm and hand position. Be sure that your forearm is placed on the edge of the guitar just above the bridge base.

Practice both the solo and accompaniment parts in *Harvest*. The solo part begins in the 2nd position.

HARVEST

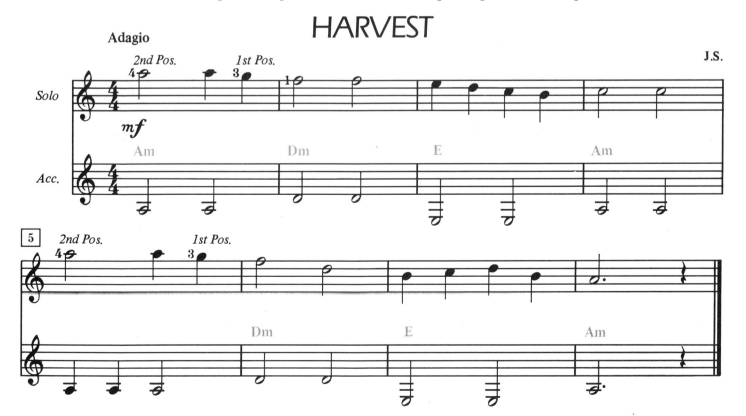

EIGHTH NOTES

Beam

Count: 1 an
Tap: down up

fig. 1 Eighth notes.

An **EIGHTH NOTE** receives one-half of a count or beat. It can be played on the *down* or on the *up* part of the beat. Eighth notes are commonly played in pairs and are attached with a beam.

Eighth notes move twice as fast as quarter notes. Count them by inserting the word ''an'' between the numbers. For example, 1 an 2 an 3 an 4 an (fig. 2).

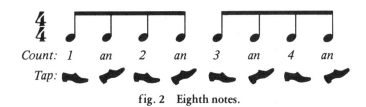

Count: 1 an 2 an 3 an 4 an
Tap:

fig. 2 Eighth notes.

PLAYING TECHNIQUES

Pickstyle. Use an *up-stroke (∨)* with the pick on eighth notes that occur on the upbeat (an). In playing the *up-stroke*, the index finger pushes the pick through the string. Follow through only enough to finish picking the string and then return to the starting point. Remember to use a minimum of movement. Use *alternate (⊓ ∨) down* and *up-strokes* when you are playing a succession of eighth notes. Use the *down-stroke* (⊓) on the down-beats and the *up-stroke* (∨) on the upbeats.

Fingerstyle. Alternate the middle and index fingers using the *rest stroke*. When crossing strings, attempt to use the index finger on the lower (sounding) string. Move to the higher (sounding) string with the middle finger. For example, if you are playing on the 3rd string, try to create an alternating pattern that allows you to move to the 2nd string with the middle finger. Conversely, if you are playing on the 2nd string, try to move to the 3rd string with the index finger.

Practice the following exercises using either the *pickstyle* or *fingerstyle* technique. Play the rhythm patterns on various open and fretted strings.

ODE TO JOY

L. Beethoven

Are You Sleeping is a round. Each guitarist should play the song twice. The 2nd guitarist begins at the beginning of the song when the 1st guitarist reaches Ⓐ.

ARE YOU SLEEPING?

Round

For additional practice playing eighth notes, play the solo part of *Chord Study* on page 28.

In popular music language, *lead* has become a synonym for melody or solo. A lead guitar player plays the solo or melodic material in a song.

ROCKIN' OUT (lead)

Rhythm Guitar

Pickstyle. When strumming eighth note patterns, it is only necessary to strum the 1st and 2nd strings on the *up-stroke* (V), fig. 1.

Fingerstyle (strumming). Use the brush or finger strum as described on page 24. When strumming an *up-strum* (↑), strike the 1st and 2nd strings with the fleshy part of the index finger, fig. 2.

Since rhythm patterns are often repeated several times, an abbreviated *slash* notation is often used to notate rhythm guitar parts, fig. 3.

fig. 1 Pickstyle.   fig. 2 Fingerstyle.   fig. 3 Slash notation.

Practice the following rhythm patterns on the open 3rd, 2nd, and 1st strings (Em chord). Count out loud as you strum. Tap your foot on the down beats. Use either the pickstyle or fingerstyle approach. Better yet, learn to do both. Remember to play only the 1st and 2nd strings on the *up-strokes*.

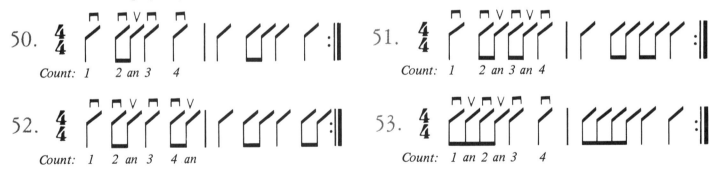

The following rhythm guitar part can be played with the lead line of *Rockin' Out*. When you do not have another guitarist to play with, use a tape recorder. A tape recording can be a great aid in learning to play the guitar. Record the rhythm guitar part to *Rockin' Out* and practice the lead with your recording.

ROCKIN' OUT (rhythm)

G and D⁷ Chords 4 strings

The open 4th string D can be added to the **G** and **D7** chords.

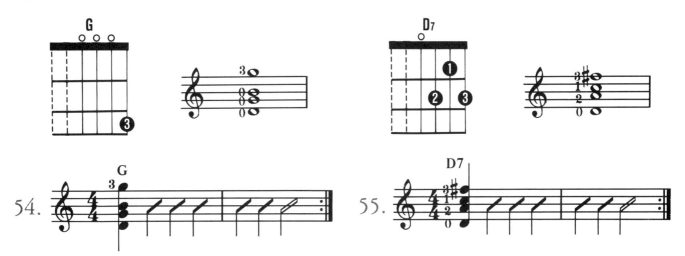

Rock rhythm patterns are developed from eighth note rhythm patterns. It is important to learn how to play "straight eighths"; that is, eighth notes that are even, in strict tempo, and are exactly on the down and upbeats of the measure. Either pickstyle or fingerstyle techniques may be used to play the rhythm guitar part of *G Jam*.

Pickstyle. Strum four down-strokes in the 1st measure and then start playing down and up-strokes in the 2nd measure. Keep the rhythm even. When you play the up-stroke, it is only necessary to strum the 1st three strings (treble strings) with the pick. This technique makes the up-strokes lighter in sound than the down-strokes and helps to give you a more solid beat.

Fingerstyle (strumming). The technique is the same as the pickstyle approach except that you use the index finger to strum the strings. The fingernail strikes the strings on the down-strums (↓) and the fleshy part of the index finger strikes the treble strings on the up-strum (↑).

G JAM (rhythm)

J.S.

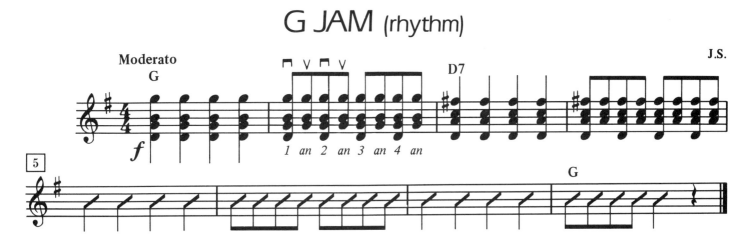

The following lead guitar part can be played with the rhythm part of *G Jam*.

G JAM (lead)

J.S.

NOTES ON THE FOURTH STRING

E 2nd fret, 4th string

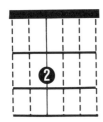

The **E** is located on the 4th string, 2nd fret. Use the 2nd finger to fret the note. Play exercises 56 and 57 with a pick (⊓), the thumb (free stroke) or the fingers (*i, m*—rest strokes).

For additional practice in playing the E, play the solo part to *Minor Toot* on page 27.

Em Chord 4 strings

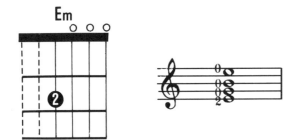

The E on the 4th string can be added to the **Em CHORD**. Keep the 2nd finger arched so that it does not touch the open 3rd string. Strum the chord with a pick, the index finger or the thumb. Play exercise 58.

C Chord 4 strings

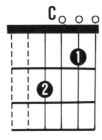
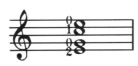

To play the **C CHORD** (4 strings), place the middle finger on the 2nd fret, 4th string and the index finger on the 1st fret, 2nd string. Keep the fingers arched to avoid touching the open 3rd and 1st strings.

Rhythm Guitar

Review the G and D7 chords (page 41) and then play exercise 61. Practice fingering the G chord with the 4th finger as well as with the 3rd finger. Strum the chords with a pick, the index finger or the thumb.

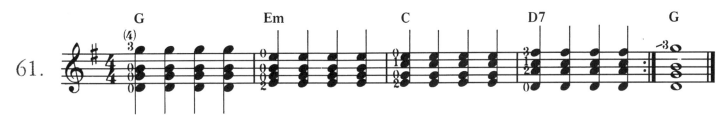

Strum exercise 62 with alternating down-up strokes with a pick or with the index finger.

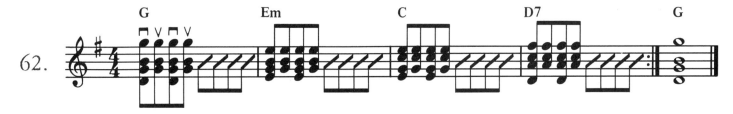

In exercise 63, the 2nd upbeat (2 *an*) is TIED to the 3rd downbeat (3). Do not strum the chord on the 3rd downbeat. DROP the chord strum out of the pattern but continue the down-up motion of the pick or index finger. Just avoid strumming the strings on the 3rd downbeat. Give a little accent (>) or emphasis to the 2nd upbeat (2 *an*).

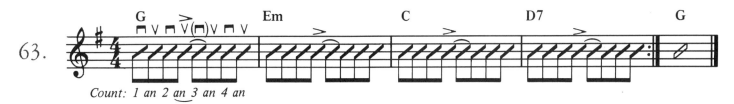

Lead Guitar

The following lead patterns or **RIFFS** (short melodies) can be played with exercises 61, 62, and 63. Have a friend or your teacher play the rhythm guitar chords as you play the lead patterns.

Pickstyle. Alternate the pick on the eighth notes. Use a down-stroke on the downbeats (numbers) and an up-stroke on the upbeats (an).

Fingerstyle. In general, alternate the index and middle fingers with rest strokes. Occasionally you will use a repeated pattern to facilitate the crossing of strings.

Bass-Chord Patterns: D⁷ and G⁷

Use a down-stroke with a pick or a free stroke with the thumb on the open 4th string (D). Strum the chord with a pick or with the index finger. In exercises 70 and 71, accent (>) the 2nd and 4th downbeats of the measure. Notice that in exercise 71, you use two down-strokes on the eighth notes.

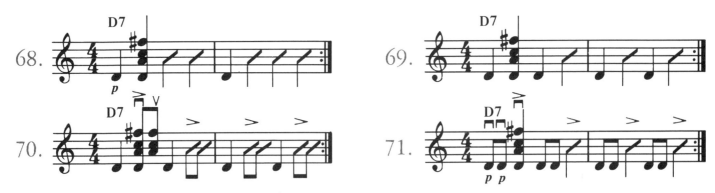

The G7 chord (3 strings) was introduced on page 28. The open D, 4th string can be added to this chord. Exercise 72 includes the bass-chord patterns for the **G7 CHORD** (4 strings).

A⁷ Chord full

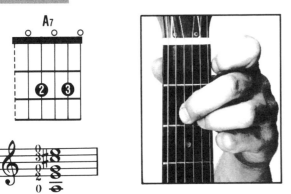

The **A7 CHORD** has a C sharp (C♯) in it. The C♯ is located on the 2nd fret, 2nd string. Use the 2nd and 3rd fingers to fret this chord. It is the best fingering to use when going to the D7 chord.

Bass-Chord Pattern: A⁷

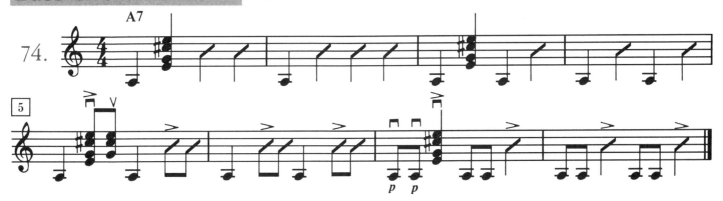

For additional practice in playing the G, C, G7, D7, and A7 chords, play the chord changes to *Easy Rock* on page 14, *Comin' Out Rock* on page 16, *Mary Ann* on page 18, and *Jingle Bells* on page 22. Record the melodies of these songs and play the chords with your recording. Begin by playing a chord on each beat in the measure.

The A7 and D7 chords have a similar shape. In both chords, the 2nd and 3rd fingers are located on the 2nd fret. Get in the habit of *lifting* and *placing* the fingers together. Keep the movement of the fingers at an absolute minimum.

PLAYING TECHNIQUES

Pickstyle. Stroke the bass notes with two successive down-strokes and then strum the chord. Give emphasis to the 2nd and 4th beats of the measure.

Fingerstyle. Pluck the bass notes with the thumb and then strum the chord with the index finger. Accent (>) the 2nd and 4th beats of the measure.

Before you attempt to play the rhythm guitar part for *Celebrate*, practice the chord progression, giving one down strum for each downbeat in the measure.

CELEBRATE (rhythm)

For additional practice in playing this chord progression, turn back to page 16 and play the rhythm guitar part to *Comin' Out Rock*.

The following lead guitar part can be played with the rhythm guitar part of *Celebrate*. Record one part and practice the other part with it.

CELEBRATE (lead)

ARPEGGIOS (broken chords)

Arpeggio—let each note ring.

An **ARPEGGIO** is a *broken chord*. Individual notes of the chord are picked or plucked and allowed to *sustain* or *ring* into the next note. This produces the sound of a chord—but one note at a time.

PLAYING TECHNIQUE

Pickstyle. There is essentially no new technique to learn. Other than the fact that you will be changing from one string to another more frequently, the pickstyle technique of down-strokes on the down beats and up-strokes on the up beats remains the same.

Fingerstyle. The hand position is the same as that used to play chords (see page 25). *Plant* the hand and use *free strokes*. The thumb is used on the lowest (sounding) chord tones and the fingers pluck the other chord tones.

Am and E Chord 3 strings

To play the **A minor (Am) CHORD**, the fingers must be arched and *almost* on the tips to avoid touching adjacent strings. Keep your left hand fingernails short. The **E CHORD** contains a **G sharp**. The **G♯** is located on the 1st fret, 3rd string.

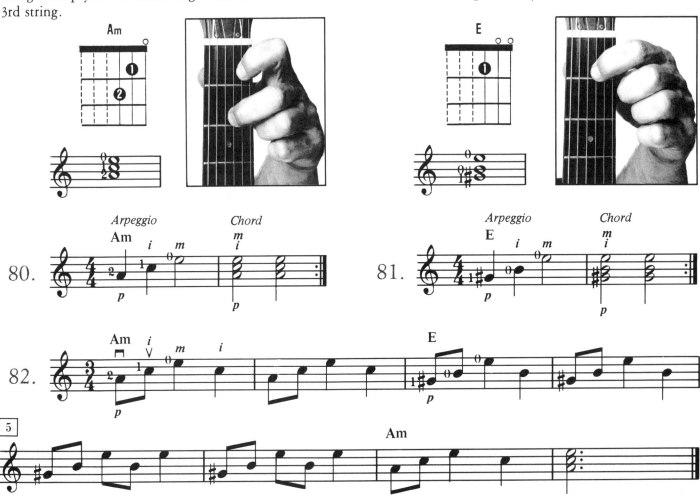

Learn to play the solo and accompaniment parts to *Daybreak*. Remember to slightly stress the 1st beat of the measure in three-quarter time.

DAYBREAK

J.S.

Dm Chord 3 strings

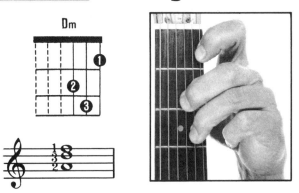

To play the **D minor (Dm) CHORD**, place the index finger on the 1st fret, 1st string, the 2nd finger on the 2nd fret, 3rd string and the 3rd finger on the 3rd fret, 2nd string.

Am ETUDE

J.S.

Basic Fingerstyle Hand Position

In order to include the 3rd or ring finger, the right hand position needs to be expanded. The symbol used to indicate the 3rd or ring finger is *a* for anular. The fingers are used to pluck the **TREBLE** (3rd, 2nd, and 1st) strings and the thumb is used to pluck the **BASS** (6th, 5th, and 4th) strings.

FINGERS. Place the index (*i*) finger on the 3rd string, the middle (*m*) finger on the 2nd string and the ring (*a*) finger on the 1st string. The fingers should be stacked or bunched together, fig 1.

THUMB. Place the thumb (*p*) on one of the bass strings. The thumb should be rigid and straight and should extend toward the guitar fingerboard so that it is not on a collision course with the fingers, fig. 2.

fig. 1   Hand position.

fig. 2   Hand position from underneath.

Em Chord Fingerstyle

fig. 3   Em chord—fingerstyle.

The **Em CHORD** and **ARPEGGIO** (broken chord) can be played on the OPEN strings. The thumb plucks the 6th string and the fingers pluck the treble strings. It is important to *plant* the right hand before you play. The plant usually has to be done very quickly. Use *free strokes* with the thumb and fingers as you play exercises 84–90.

*NOTE: The exercises above can also be played with a pick. Use the *strum* version of the Em chord when necessary, fig. 4.

fig. 4

Dm Chord full

The **Dm CHORD** was introduced as a 3-string chord on page 47. In order to play the full Dm chord, add the open 4th string (D). Use the thumb (*p*) on the 4th string and the fingers of the treble strings in the basic fingerstyle hand position.

The open bass strings can be added to the 3-string **Am** and **E CHORDS**. Add the A, 5th string to the Am and the open E, 6th string to the E chord. Use your fingers as indicated or play exercises 92 and 93 with a pick.

Remember to *plant* the right hand in position when you are playing fingerstyle.

PLAYING TECHNIQUES

Pickstyle. *Classical Study* can be played with a pick. Use down-strokes on the bass-chord patterns and alternating down-up strokes on the arpeggios.

Fingerstyle. Use the thumb on the open bass strings and the index, middle, and ring fingers on the 3rd, 2nd, and 1st strings. Use free strokes.

CLASSICAL STUDY

Try playing the accompaniment part for the *Prelude* on page 17 and *Spanish Song* on page 36.

F 3rd fret, 4th string

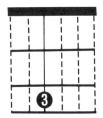

3rd finger

1st space

The **F** is located on the 3rd fret, 4th string and is fingered with the 3rd finger.

95.

REVIEW: Notes on the 4th string

The open D, 4th string was first introduced on page 37. The E on the 4th string, 2nd fret was presented on page 42. Both notes have been used in various chords.

For additional practice on playing the notes on the 4th string, turn back to page 22 and play the accompaniment to *Study*.

Learn both the solo and accompaniment parts for *Andantino*. Both parts can be played either pickstyle or fingerstyle. The solo part has been created from arpeggios. Let the notes ring. Andantino is also used as a tempo marking in music. It indicates a tempo that is slightly faster than andante.

ANDANTINO

M. Carcassi

The solo part of *Saint James Infirmary* can be played with down-strokes with a pick or with rest strokes with the fingers (*i*, *m*). Play the accompaniment part with a pick or with free strokes with the thumb.

SAINT JAMES INFIRMARY

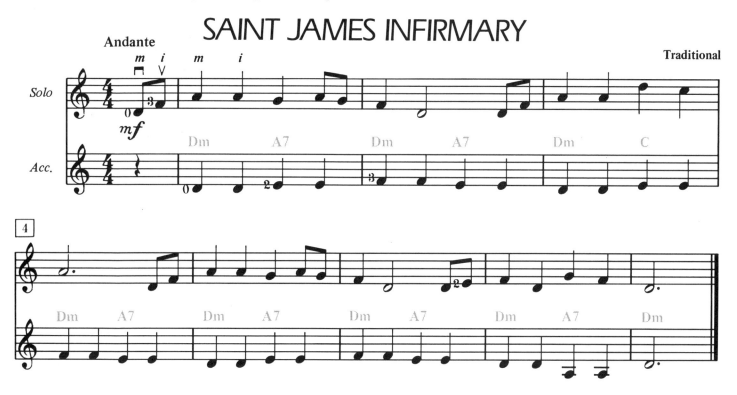

Iberia can be played with a pick or with the fingers. In fingerstyle, play the solo part with alternating *i* and *m* (rest strokes) or with the thumb (free strokes). Use the basic hand position for the accompaniment (see page 48).

IBERIA

Flats

A **FLAT** (♭) placed before a note *lowers* the note one half step. If the note is *fingered*, play the next lower note or fret, fig. 1. If the note is located on an *open* string, play the 4th fret of the next lower string unless the string is the 3rd string, then play the 3rd fret, fig. 2.

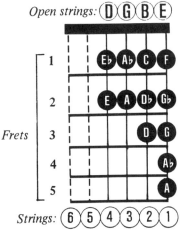

fig. 1   Flatting fingered notes.

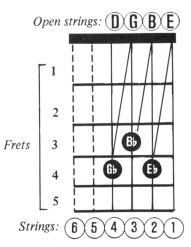

fig. 2   Flatting open string notes.

Enharmonics. This is the term used to describe tones that are actually one and the same, but are *named* and *written* differently. For example, D♯ and E♭ are the same tone even though they are written differently. Study and play exercise 99. Review sharps (♯) on page 30.

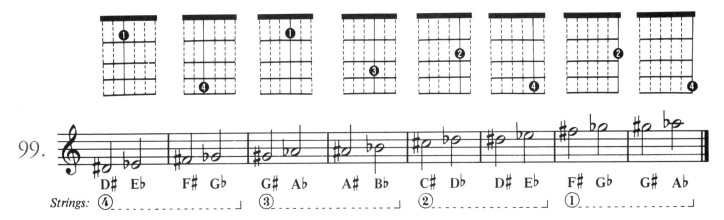

Chromatic Scale

A **CHROMATIC SCALE** is a scale in which each successive note is a *half step* apart (see page 30). Exercise 100 is the **G Chromatic Scale.** It begins on the open G, 3rd string and moves by half steps up to the G, 1st string, 3rd fret. Sharps (♯) are used on the ascending chromatic scale and flats (♭) are used when the scale descends.

Left Hand Playing Technique. When playing the *descending scale,* it is helpful to *plant* the index finger of the left hand on the fingerboard in *preparation* for the note it will fret. For example, as you move from the 1st string to the 2nd string, place the index finger immediately on the 1st fret, 2nd string (C) as you fret the E♭ with the little finger. This promotes a good hand position, speed, and accuracy. After you have played the open 2nd string (B), plant the index finger on the 1st fret, 3rd string (A♭) as you fret the B♭ with the ring finger.

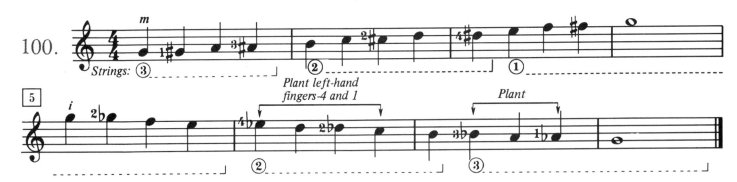

Tied Eighth Note Rhythms

As you have learned, a **TIE** is used to connect two notes of the *same pitch* (see page 18). When a tie is used with quarter, half, or whole notes, it generally extends the note value across the bar line into the next measure. The tie is also used within the same measure to tie eighth notes that occur on the upbeat (*an*) to a quarter or half note. This results in rhythms that are commonly found in pop, jazz, and rock music.

Syncopation. In 4/4 time, the normal accent (>) is on the 1st beat of the measure with the secondary accent on the 3rd beat (ex. 101). To accent a note means to stress one tone over others. When the accent is shifted to a normally weak beat, it is called *syncopation* (ex. 102). Play these two exercises on the open 1st string (E). Play the accented note a little louder.

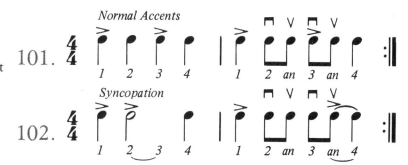

The tied eighth note rhythms found in *Groovin'* are examples of syncopation. In preparation for playing the solo part, practice the following rhythm exercises on the open 1st string (E). Use a pick or alternate the index and middle fingers (rest strokes).

Groovin' contains two FLATS: A♭ on the 1st string in measure 4 and A♭ on the 3rd string in measure 8. You have previously played those notes as their *enharmonic* equivalent—G♯.

GROOVIN' (lead)

J.S.

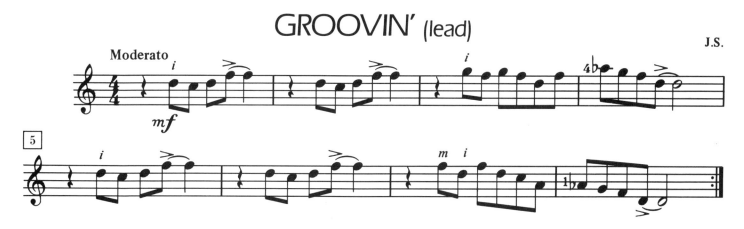

Rock rhythms are often based on a down-stroke motion. Play the accompaniment bass line to *Groovin'* with successive down-strokes with a pick. Slightly **MUTE** the strings by allowing the heel of the right hand to rest on the strings at the bridge. This will give you a "chucking" sound. It is possible to play this part with the thumb but it is not as effective.

GROOVIN' (rhythm-bass)

J.S.

NOTES ON THE FIFTH STRING

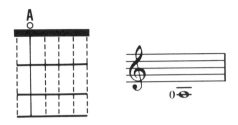

The **OPEN A, 5th STRING** was introduced on page 37. **B** is located on the 2nd fret and is fingered with the 2nd finger. **C** is located on the 3rd fret. Use the 3rd finger to fret this note.

Practice the following exercises using either a down-stroke with a pick, free strokes with the thumb, or alternating rest strokes with the index and middle fingers.

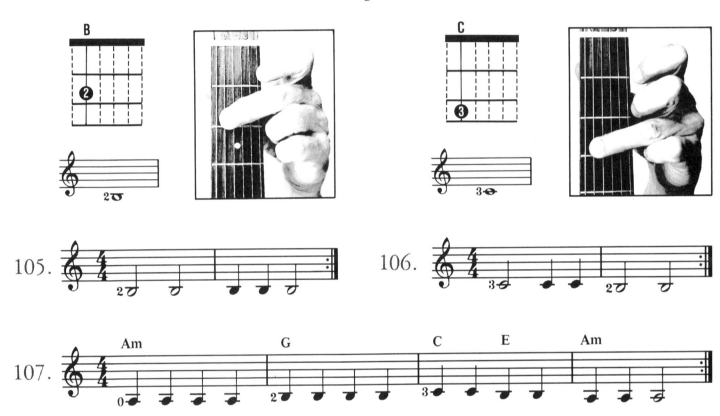

Shout has a rhythm bass line that is similar to the one used in *Groovin'* except that it starts on the A, open 5th string. Use successive down-strokes with a pick and *mute* the strings with the heel of the right hand (see page 53).

SHOUT (rhythm-bass)

J.S.

When you have learned the rhythm-bass part to *Shout*, make a recording of it. Practice the lead line with your recording. Keep it at a slow tempo until you can play the lead line without any hesitation or errors.

SHOUT (lead)

J.S.

Power Chords
rhythm guitar

The **A5**, **D5**, and **E5** rock **POWER CHORDS** can be used for the rhythm-bass part of *Shout*. Each chord is a two note chord. Use the index finger to fret the string as well as to damp (⊗) the adjacent (high in pitch) strings. The most effective playing technique is to use successive down-strokes with a pick as you *mute* the strings with the heel of your hand.

SHOUT (power chords)

J.S

*A partial C chord is used in measures 2 and 6.

If you are using a pick, use down-strokes for each note in *Gypsy Nights*. Fingerstyle players have two options: play the notes on the bass strings with the thumb and the notes on the treble strings with the fingers, using free strokes; or, play all of the notes with the index and middle fingers (alternating), using rest strokes. Notice the F♯, 4th string in measure 8.

GYPSY NIGHTS

For additional practice in playing the F♯ on the 4th string, play the solo part of *Night Journey* on page 27 and the accompaniment part for *Meditation* on page 29.

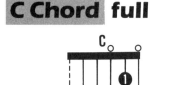 **full**

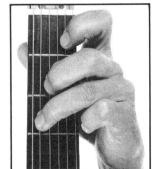

This is a full **C CHORD**. Avoid touching the open 3rd and 1st strings. Keep the fingers arched and the fingernails short. Strum the chord with a pick or the index finger.

Here is a solo version of *Rhody*. This type of guitar solo, with the melody in the bass along with accompaniment chords, is called the CARTER STYLE, after the Carter family. Use down-strokes with the pick or pluck the bass notes (melody) with the thumb and strum or pluck the chords.

RHODY (solo)

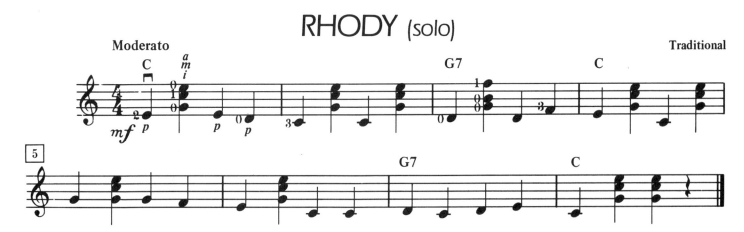

More Enharmonic Notes

As mentioned on page 52, **ENHARMONIC** notes are the same note but they are named and written differently. For example, A♯ and B♭ on the 5th string, 1st fret are enharmonic notes. The C♯ and D♭ located on the 5th string, 4th fret are one and the same.

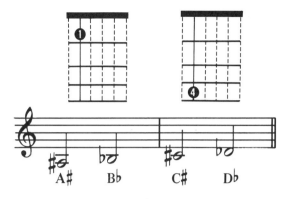

Enharmonic notes.

A Chromatic Scale

The **A Chromatic Scale** moves by half steps from the open A, 5th string up to the A on the 3rd string, 2nd fret. As you descend, use the *planting* technique described on page 52.

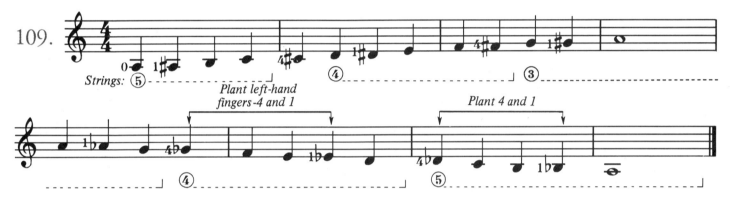

Chord/Bass Note Em/D

To indicate the *lowest* note of a chord, a slash (/) and the name of the note can be added after the chord name. For example, Em/D means to play an Em chord with a D in the bass. *Nuage* contains several examples of this chord/bass notation. This song also provides you with additional practice in playing sharps. Learn both the solo and accompaniment parts. In the accompaniment part, use the basic hand position (free strokes) or use a pick with alternating down and up-strokes. Let the notes in the accompaniment part ring. They are arpeggios or broken chords.

Natural Signs (♮). Natural signs are used to cancel or eliminate sharps and flats. The *bar line* also cancels sharps or flats that may have been added to the previous measure. In measure 2 of *Nuage*, the natural sign is added as a reminder. It is placed in parenthesis because the bar line has already canceled the D♯ that was added in measure 1.

NUAGE

J.S.

NOTES ON THE SIXTH STRING

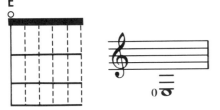

The **OPEN E, 6th STRING** has been used in several songs and exercises since its introduction on page 37. Two additional notes on the 6th string are **F** and **G**. The F is located on the 1st fret and is fingered with the 1st finger. The G is located on the 3rd fret and is fingered with the 3rd finger.

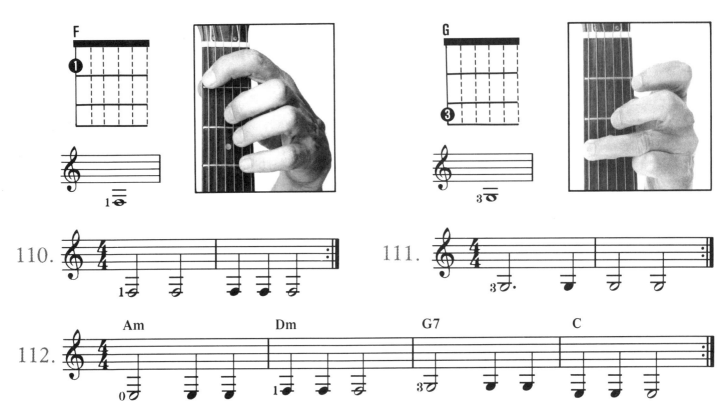

For additional practice, play the accompaniment part to *B-C Mix* on page 13, *Breezin'* on page 15, *Folk Song* on page 34, and *Ode To Joy* on page 39.

Learn both the solo and accompaniment parts to *Sleeper's Wake*. Play the accompaniment part with a pick or with free strokes with the thumb.

SLEEPER'S WAKE (theme)

J.S. Bach

Walking Bass

A **WALKING BASS** line moves by step or by small skips from one chord tone to another. The rhythm is usually successive quarter notes; that is, one note for every beat in the measure.

Rhythm Guitar

E⁷ Chord 4 strings

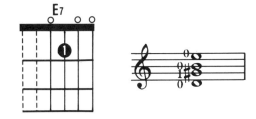

To play the **E7 CHORD**, place the tip of the index finger on the 1st fret, 3rd string. Strum or pluck the 4th, 3rd, 2nd, and 1st strings. Practice exercises 114 and 115, then play the rhythm guitar part for the walking bass line presented above.

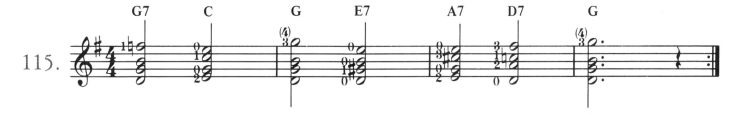

Dotted Quarter Note

When a DOT is added to a quarter note, it adds a half beat (½) to the value of the note. A **DOTTED QUARTER NOTE** receives one and one-half beats (1 + ½ = 1½).

The dotted quarter note is most often used in a **DOTTED QUARTER-EIGHTH NOTE** rhythm pattern. This pattern exists in the beginning of two familiar songs, *London Bridge* and *Deck the Halls*.

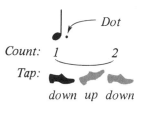

Dotted quarter note.

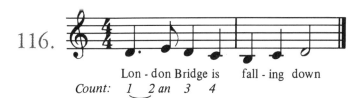

The dotted quarter-eighth note rhythm introduced on page 59 is used in measure 3 of *Scarborough Fair*.

SCARBOROUGH FAIR

F Chord inside strings

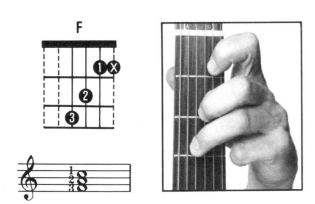

The **F CHORD** is played on the inside strings. Omit the 1st string from the chord. Damp (❌) the 1st string with the side of the index finger.

Some chords have been added to create a chord solo arrangement of *Scarborough Fair*. Review the Dm chord on page 49 and the C chord on page 56. Use a pick or the basic fingerstyle hand position to play this solo.

SCARBOROUGH FAIR (solo)

G Chord full

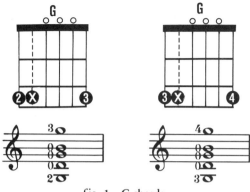

fig. 1   G chords.

The full **G CHORD** has several common fingerings. You need to know them all. The fingering you use depends upon the chord that you are playing before and after the G chord. Fig. 1 illustrates a good beginning G chord. Damp (prevent from sounding) the open 5th string by lightly touching it with the finger that is fretting the 6th string. The G chords diagramed in fig. 2 are optional fingerings. In these G chords, the 5th string is included.

fig. 2   G chords

Pickstyle. Play the eighth notes with alternating down-up strokes with the pick.

Fingerstyle. Alternate the index and middle fingers on the lead. In the accompaniment, strum the chords and pluck the bass notes with the thumb.

BLUES ROCK

*Fermata Sign (⌒). Also known as a hold, the fermata sign tells the player to sustain a note or chord about double (but not exactly) the normal value.

D Chord full

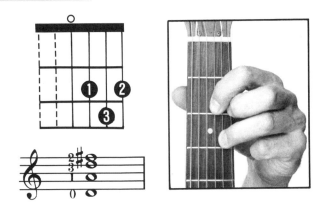

Arch the 3rd finger to avoid touching the 1st string when playing the **D CHORD**.

To play the accompaniment part of *Country Rock*, pick or pluck the bass note on the 1st beat of the measure and strum the chord on *2 an 3*. Review the chords used in this song: G, D, Em, and C.

COUNTRY ROCK

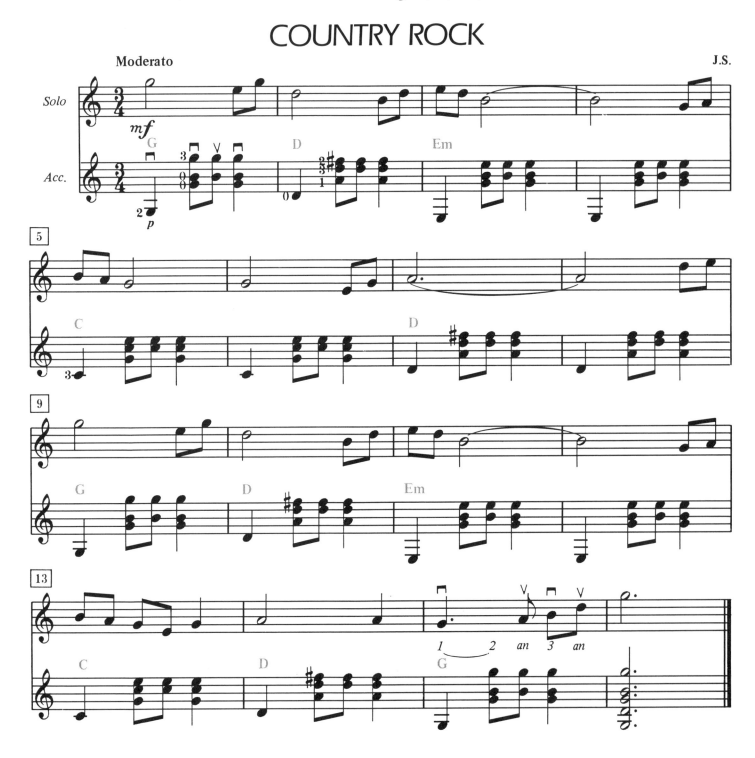

2/4 Time Signature

The 2/4 **TIME SIGNATURE** organizes the rhythm of the music into two beats per measure. The 1st beat of the measure should receive more emphasis or stress. Count 1 2 1 2.

$\mathbf{\frac{2}{4}}$ = Two beats in each measure
= A quarter note receives one beat

Review the dotted quarter note rhythm on page 59. Play the melody of *House Of The Rising Sun* pickstyle or fingerstyle with the thumb. When the melody moves to the 3rd string, you have the option of using the thumb or fingers. Use free strokes.

HOUSE OF THE RISING SUN

The following arrangement adds chords (harmony) to the melody. While this arrangement is playable both pick and fingerstyle, it is best suited as a pickstyle arrangement. The melody is once again in the bass line with occasional chords. Since the song moves at a slow tempo, everything can be played with down strokes.

HOUSE OF THE RISING SUN (solo)

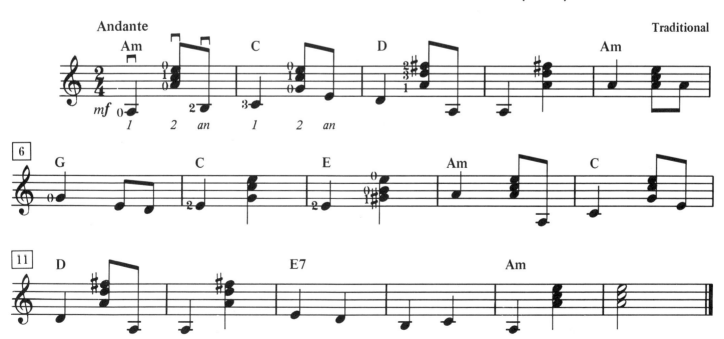

E⁶ and A⁶ Chords

The **E6** and **A6** are used in the accompaniment part of *Rhythm 'n' Blues*. These chords, fig. 1 and 2, are extensions of the *power chords* introduced on page 55.

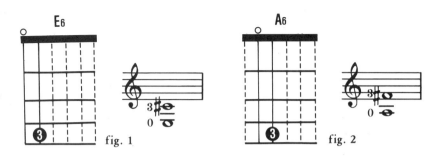

Practice exercises 120 and 121. Since you are going back and forth between the power chords (E5, A5) and the 6 chord (E6, A6), leave your index finger in place (in this case, on the 2nd fret).

RHYTHM 'n' BLUES